Shanleya's
QUEST

A Botany
Adventure
for Kids
Ages 9 to 99

Written by Thomas J. Elpel
Illustrated by Gloria Brown

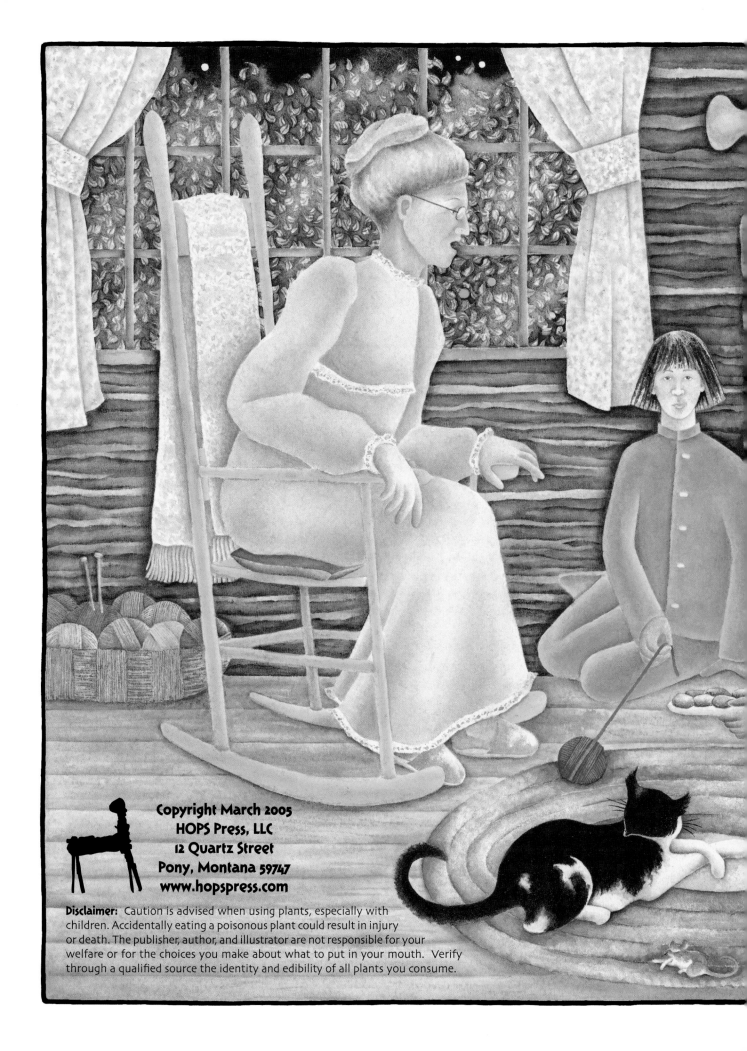

STORY TIME

"Grandma, tell us the story of Shanleya," the children begged.

"Yes," said Katlyn, "we want to hear about her island adventures."

"I want to hear how Shanleya tricked the Guardians," Peter chimed in.

"And I want to know what happened to the Great Tree," Adelia added.

Outside, the cool night wind rustled the leaves on the trees and filtered in through little cracks in the lodge. Peter added wood to the fire, while Grandmother set out a plate of her delicious cookies.

"I will tell you the story of Shanleya," the old woman said, "but we must start at the very beginning. Come closer so I don't have to talk so loud."

The children eagerly shared the cookies and scooted closer to hear her story.

THE RAIN OF TIME

Father Sun and Mother Moon smiled at their newborn ball of molten rock spinning slowly in space below them. "Our child is so beautiful," said Father Sun.

"Yes," said Mother Moon, "but there is something missing. Without the passage of Time our little Earth will never grow and change from what she is right now."

No one had ever made Time before, but they thought and thought, until Father Sun had an idea. He reached out and squeezed water from the skies over Earth. "Let's make Time a liquid," he said, "and the liquid will fall as rain to mark the passage of Time."

So it began to rain Time on the Earth, cooling the surface of this molten ball to make solid ground. Raindrops flowed together forming little streams and then bigger rivers, rolling downhill to become great puddles in the lowest places on Earth. Drop by drop, moment by moment, the puddles began to grow.

Every day Father Sun beamed his light and love down upon Earth. Every night Mother Moon kept the nightlight on, gently glowing over her child below. While they kept watch from above, there were things happening on Earth that even they did not know about. The rain of Time washed minerals and natural chemicals off the landscape into the growing puddles, creating a most peculiar soup. Without heat or light, these puddles would have been nothing more than puddles. But Father Sun's warmth charged the soup with energy. Like a witch's cauldron, strange things formed and bubbled to the surface.

SOUP BUBBLES

You might not expect much from bubbles in a puddle of soup, but all the light and love from Father Sun above charged the bubbles to attract matter, causing them to grow and grow until they nearly popped. But instead of popping, one little bubble split in half to become two identical smaller bubbles.

The new bubbles were charged by Father Sun's energy, attracting some minerals and chemicals like magnets drawn together, while repelling other matter like magnets turned the opposite way. The bubbles grew as big as the first one until they also split, and the two bubbles became four.

The four grew and split to make eight then the eight became sixteen. The rain of Time continued to fall, and the soup was soon filled with itsy-bitsy, teensy tinsy, very little bubbles that were all identical, or almost identical.

With so many ingredients in the soup, some bubbles attracted unique combinations of materials and formed slightly different, slightly flawed bubbles. Usually they just popped, but sometimes a flawed bubble was as good as or better than the original. It grew and split, making endless copies of a new kind of bubble.

Father Sun and Mother Moon knew nothing of this mayhem from their perches in the sky. Their little Earth seemed to nap quietly below, while the rain of Time puddled deeper and deeper, forming first lakes and then oceans.

Just imagine trying to fill an ocean with a garden hose, and you can sense the incredible patience of Father Sun and Mother Moon as they watched over their sleeping child.

"Look! What's that?" Father Sun exclaimed after what seemed like an eternity of quiet waiting.

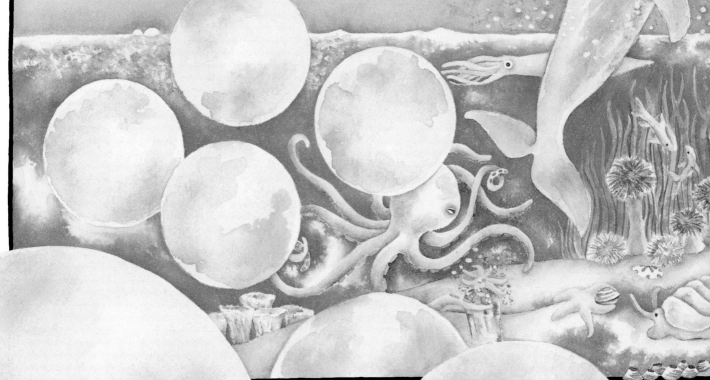

"What is what?" wondered Mother Moon, startled by his sudden outburst.

"The water that was once blue is now almost green," replied Father Sun, and they peered closer to see that the oceans were full of life. What were once invisibly small bubbles floating in Time had copied and recopied themselves through so many millions of generations and through so many flaws, that they were no longer just bubbles, but truly living organisms.

Near the surface floated tiny green plants that absorbed Father Sun's great warmth, using the energy much as the bubbles once did to latch onto the nutrient chemicals needed to grow and split into still more and more copies.

Swimming in the water were animated lifeforms that absorbed the plants for the nutrients and energy they contained. And other animated life forms followed them, consuming the creatures that consumed the plants. Earth was alive in a spectacular way, and Mother Moon and Father Sun watched in stunned fascination from above.

Life filled the oceans, then spilled over onto bare ground, with plants taking root in the soil, while the animals that ate them adapted and followed the food into this new habitat.

Overhead, the rain of Time continued to shower down upon the landscape, raising the oceans ever so slowly, drop by drop, minute by minute, century by century. But what would happen when Time covered all of Earth in an endless ocean of water?

THE GREAT TREE

As Mother Moon and Father Sun watched from above, all the animals migrated in search of higher ground while the plants grew in the only direction they could to escape the water: UP. The composted and fossilized remains of each generation formed a solid mound of earth and rock to support new plants. It started out as a lowly mound soon surrounded by an ocean of Time that just kept getting deeper and deeper. But the plants reached down their roots and brought up new mineral nutrients from below, and the mound kept growing.

Generation after generation grew and died, adding more and more matter to the mound. The island grew taller as fast as the water around it grew deeper. But not every generation was identical to the one before it, as young ones seldom are. The plants mis-copied themselves, generation by generation, until those on one side of the island were different from those on the other. Each colony grew upon the remains of its ancestors, forming two separate mounds on the original one.

Through the drip-drip of Time the water level rose higher and higher until it filled the channel between the two mounds. Now there were two separate islands connected underwater by a common trunk. And so it was through eons of Time that this funny mound grew and grew, branching out this direction and that, until there were hundreds of separate islands all connected to the same great trunk, rooted to the bottom of an ocean deeper than anyone could imagine. On each island grew only the most closely related plants that had long ago branched-off from plants on the other islands.

Meanwhile, the poor animals retreated to the last remaining mountain peaks that were not underwater. Each day the gazelles and deer and buffalo, and all the other animals, swam out into the ocean in search of those little islands of greenery to feed upon. The animals could never stay very long, however, for the islands were inhabited by Guardians—protectors of the islands. Some Guardians were friendly by day, but at night they all came out to hunt. So the animals ate what they could by day and swam back to dry land to sleep at night.

SHANLEYA

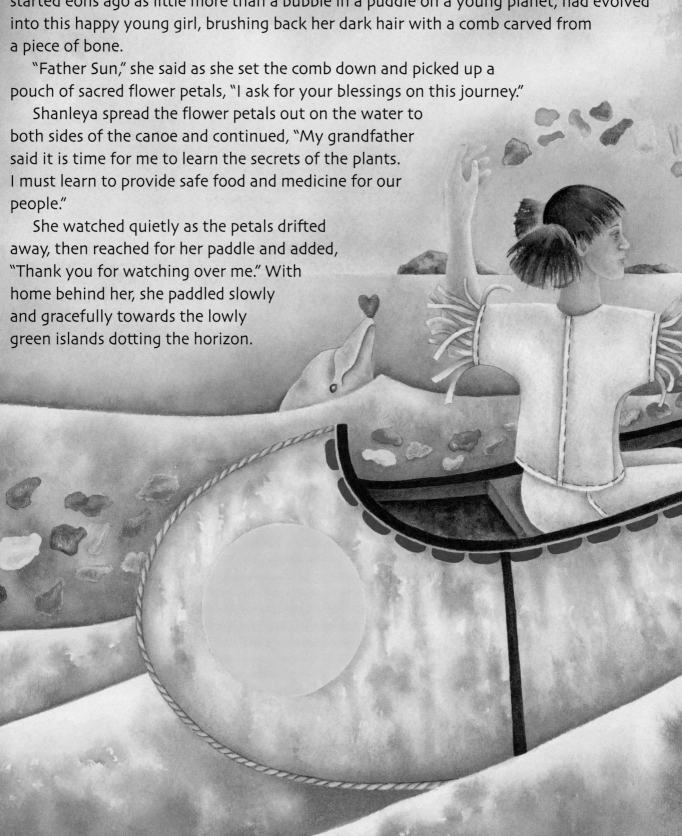

It is early in the morning here in this waterworld that we meet Shanleya gazing at the reflection of her earth-toned skin and sky blue eyes in the water beside her canoe. What started eons ago as little more than a bubble in a puddle on a young planet, had evolved into this happy young girl, brushing back her dark hair with a comb carved from a piece of bone.

"Father Sun," she said as she set the comb down and picked up a pouch of sacred flower petals, "I ask for your blessings on this journey."

Shanleya spread the flower petals out on the water to both sides of the canoe and continued, "My grandfather said it is time for me to learn the secrets of the plants. I must learn to provide safe food and medicine for our people."

She watched quietly as the petals drifted away, then reached for her paddle and added, "Thank you for watching over me." With home behind her, she paddled slowly and gracefully towards the lowly green islands dotting the horizon.

FINDING MINT ISLAND

"You must find Mint Island," Shanleya remembered Grandfather's words in her mind, "and bring back the spices that make our food taste so good."

There were more than three hundred islands out there, each inhabited by a different family of closely related plants. Grandfather gave the eager youngster a map to steer her towards Mint Island, which she had to correctly identify from the other islands around it. "Look for square stems and opposite leaves," Grandfather told her, "and be sure to smell the plants. Most of them have a spicy, minty aroma."

Shanleya had no doubts when she found Mint Island. She smelled the sweet and spicy herbs on the morning breeze long before reaching shore. The girl tied her canoe to a sturdy clump of mints at the water's edge and grabbed her collecting bag. She identified mint, peppermint, and spearmint by smell alone. Still, she checked the plants to be safe and yes, they had square stems and opposite leaves just as Grandfather said they would. She admired the odd-looking irregular flowers too.

"Good morning, Miss." Shanleya jumped at the sound of the voice behind her, and turned around to meet the Guardian of Mint Island. He stood straight and square with a red-and-white striped candy cane for a walking stick and a stately crown of wild bergamot flowers upon his head. Shanleya knew immediately that this Guardian was among the friendliest she would ever meet.

"Sorry to startle you!" he apologized, handing her a candied mint leaf. At home Shanleya often helped her mother make candies just like it. They dipped fresh mint leaves in a thick syrup and dried them in the sun.

"Oh, thank you," said the girl as she popped the treat in her mouth to suck on. "My name is Shanleya. Grandfather sent me here to learn about all the plants on Mint Island. Could you show me around?"

"I would be happy to show you around," the Guardian said, "but I could not possibly show you ALL of the Mint Family, since there are more than 3,500 different species here." So the Guardian and the girl explored the island. To Shanleya it was like walking through her mother's spice cabinet. She recognized many spices by smell from her mother's cooking: basil, rosemary, lavender, thyme, marjoram, savory, and sage. This was culinary sage, she knew, not at all like sagebrush, which grows on another island.

"Collect only what you need," Grandfather told her before she left. "We must never waste our sacred plants." Shanleya collected a sampling of good-smelling herbs for her mother, plus a mint stalk to chew on as she travelled. She thanked the Guardian for his kindness, then returned to her canoe and paddled to the next island.

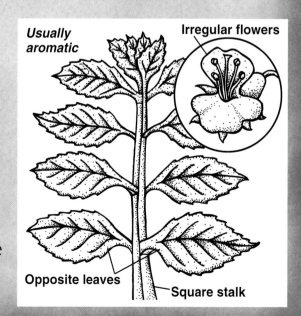

Usually aromatic

Irregular flowers

Opposite leaves

Square stalk

THE PARSLEY GUARDIAN

"Parsleys are important plants," Grandfather had said. "Like the Mints, there are great spices on Parsley Island, including fennel, celery, anise, chervil, coriander, cumin, caraway, dill, and of course, parsley." Shanleya recognized some of the names from her mother's cooking. "There are more than 3,000 different species in the Parsley Family," he told her, "including a few edibles like carrots and parsnips, but there are also some deadly plants," he cautioned her. "Only collect plants of this family when you are with an adult who can correctly pick the safe ones from the bad."

Shanleya knew she had the right island as soon as she saw the flower heads. They looked like little umbrellas, but with the spokes turned upward. Grandfather called them "umbels" she recalled. All the spokes started at exactly the same point on the end of the main stem. At the end of each spoke was another, smaller umbel. Grandfather said that a few other plants had umbels, but only the Parsleys had double umbels. He called it a "compound umbel," Shanleya recalled. Little five-petaled flowers formed on the ends of the smaller umbels, and later formed pairs of seeds.

Shanleya toured the island on foot looking at different plants of the Parsley Family. Most had little white or yellow flowers, she noticed. Then, from behind her she heard the squeaky voice of the Parsley Guardian.

"Welcome to my island young girrrl," the Guardian said in his most polite, squeaky voice. "Won't you come annd join me for some sooup?" Shanleya wanted to sprint for the canoe, but she couldn't risk provoking an attack and fumbled for a good excuse. Finding none, she nodded and followed the Guardian back to his lodge, sitting down for soup at his picnic table out front.

"What's the maaattter? Don't you truuussst me?" the Guardian squeaked, as the girl stared at her bowl. Scrambling for a way out, Shanleya pointed to a flying bird behind the Guardian. "Do you know what kind of bird that is?" she asked, then quickly but quietly switched the bowls when the Guardian turned around to look.

"Silly girrrl, how can you paddle around these islands and not-t-t know what a seagull is-s-s?" the Guardian admonished her.

"Sorry," Shanleya said. The Guardian took a slurp from his bowl. He swallowed and slurped again, but then his eyes went wide and he dropped the bowl, splattering soup everywhere, and squealed, "You poisoned meee!" He fell to the ground in convulsions and then lay still.

"Water hemlock," Shanleya thought. The soup would have killed her for sure, but the Guardian was only unconscious. Shanleya knew she would forever have to be wary of Parsley Island. She sprinted for her canoe before the beast awoke.

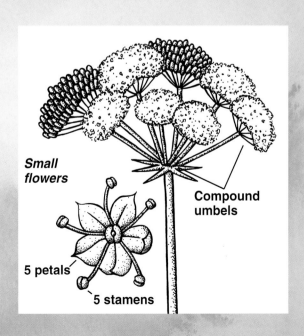

Small flowers

Compound umbels

5 petals

5 stamens

THE SECRET COMBINATION TO MUSTARD ISLAND

Mustard Island was different from the others. Shanleya recognized it by the weedy landscape and the barren patches of ground. She could see the Guardian out there with a shovel, working feverishly to turn over the soil. "The Guardian of Mustard Island is a good Guardian," Shanleya remembered Grandfather saying, "for a Guardian, that is."

Grandfather told her how the Mustards thrived in bare ground where most of the rain was lost as runoff. Moisture that did soak into the soil was soon lost to the sun and wind. The Mustards adapted to these harsh conditions with short lifecycles. The seeds sprouted easily after a rain and jumped up from the soil, quickly putting out leaves and a stem, flowers, and then seed. Like a radish, these plants grew quickly and were done and dead early in the year, while other plants were just getting started.

The Guardian saw the girl paddling towards the island and welcomed her ashore. "I have a challenge for you," he offered. "If you know the combination to Mustard Island, then you are welcome to come and collect Mustard greens any time. But if you do not know the combination, then I will ban you from this island forever."

The Guardian pointed to a pile of wooden pieces carved and painted to look like flower parts. The challenge was to put the right parts in the right order to create a model of a Mustard flower. Shanleya knew this game well, for she had played with a similar model in Grandfather's lodge for as long as she could remember. Whenever she put the model together correctly, Grandfather gave her a special treat: a spicy yellow-brown paste made from crushed mustard seeds. Shanleya like to spread the mustard paste on sandwiches of roasted gazelle and lettuce.

Most flowers start out wrapped in a bud of green or sometimes colored "sepals" that burst open to reveal the flower, Shanleya recalled. Turn a flower over and you will see the sepals hiding there. Shanleya knew that Mustards have four sepals and four petals, so she set those pieces up and put the extras back. Then she picked up the stamens.

Grandfather had told her that the stamens always "stay men" to help her remember that these were the male parts. Shanleya placed four tall stamens and two shorter ones where they belonged, then put the pistil—the female part—in the very center.

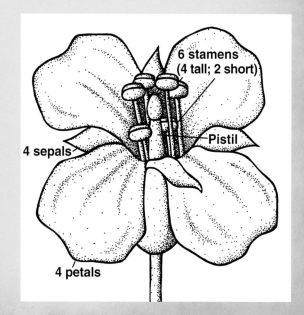

6 stamens
(4 tall; 2 short)

Pistil

4 sepals

4 petals

"Great!" said the Guardian. "That is the correct combination to every flower within the Mustard Family. There are more than 3,200 unique species here, and they are all edible, so help yourself." Shanleya gathered some mustard greens for salads, plus ripe seeds for Grandfather's mustard paste. After helping the Guardian turn over a patch of ground to grow more mustards, she gave him a hug and set out for the next island.

THE PEA ISLANDS

The Pea Islands were easy to find. The main island was covered with bright blooms, while its sister islands, Mimosa and Senna, were close enough that a person could swim the channel between them. Grandfather often told Shanleya how these islands were connected to each other through great branches underwater. Now, for the first time, she could peer down through the water and see the connecting branches herself.

The branches were said to connect these islands with all other islands to a single great trunk rooted in the ocean floor. "If you were to dive deep into the ocean," Grandfather said, "you could follow the branches back in Time to see how the plants on the different islands came from common ancestors."

Shanleya paddled directly to Pea Island. She knew exactly where to land the canoe, for the Guardian of Pea Island was proud and likable—at least during the day—and he put up a great banner at the water's edge. Beneath the banner was a dock shielded on the sides by wings made from the same cloth. It was like a Pea flower, except for one thing. To complete the flower, Shanleya paddled into the little port and tied up the canoe.

"The irregular flowers of the Peas have unique petals called the 'banner, wings and a keel,' much like the keel of a boat," Grandfather always said. "If you can recognize those petals, then you can recognize the plants of the Pea Family."

The Pea Guardian greeted Shanleya with a beautiful bouquet of sweet pea blossoms. "Welcome! Welcome!" he said. "May I show you around?"

"Yes, please do," answered the girl eagerly, and the two of them walked together. At first glance, the plants seemed very different from one another, Shanleya noted. Some were short plants, while others were sizable trees, but Shanleya noticed that the flowers all had a banner, wings, and keel, just like Grandfather had said.

"A few species are mildly poisonous," the Guardian warned her as they admired the locoweed and lupine. Finally they came to a garden of peas and beans where the sweet Guardian helped Shanleya gather enough food for a feast—peas, peanuts, pinto beans, lima beans, soybeans, cow peas, black-eyed peas, chick peas, lentils, and garbanzo beans.

After the harvest, the girl and the Guardian rested in a cozy patch of clover, searching for four-leaf clovers. Shanleya noticed that even the little clover blossoms had a banner, wings, and keel. The petals were just a bit skinnier than on the other flowers.

She could have stayed all day, but Father Sun stared down at her from high in the sky, urging her to continue the journey. It was nearly noon, and she had a long way to go. Shanleya thanked the Guardian for his time, loaded the bountiful harvest in her canoe, and paddled away.

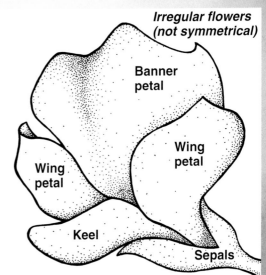

Irregular flowers (not symmetrical)

Banner petal

Wing petal

Wing petal

Keel

Sepals

The keel consists of 2 petals fused together.

THE ISLAND MAP

Shanleya spread Grandfather's tattered map on her lap. She looked at the route of where she had been, and where she had yet to go. It was a lot of paddling for one day. Grandfather wanted her to follow this route. "Learn the patterns of the plants on these islands first," he had said. "That will prepare you to study other plants later on."

Her people had developed the map over many generations. Charting the islands was the easy part. But the people could not dive deep enough in Time to see many of the connecting branches, so they looked for clues in the living plants to figure out how the islands were related. They noticed that all the islands on one side of the Great Tree shared unique features that were not found on the other islands. Shanleya paddled until she thought she was in a good place to see the difference.

"This looks like the right spot," Shanleya thought, storing the paddle in the canoe. She carefully folded the map and put it away, then ate her lunch. Mother had packed her a delicious wild goose-meat sandwich and a jar of red clover tea. From her collecting bag, the girl added mustard greens and snitched some yummy green peas. "Thank you Father Sun," Shanleya said, "for the great bounty you have provided."

Savoring the good food and the peaceful day, Shanleya stared mindlessly at the leaves floating in the water beside the canoe. It wasn't until she popped the last bite of the sandwich into her mouth that her mind woke up to what was in front of her. She scooped two leaves out of the water and studied them carefully. In one leaf the veins ran in straight rows, while in the other the veins branched out like a net.

She remembered now. Grandfather once told her that a seed from any island on the shaded left side of the map would sprout with only one leaf unfolding from the seed. He had called it a "mono-cotyle-don," meaning it had "one-seed-leaf." The plants grew with mostly straight-veined leaves, like grass.

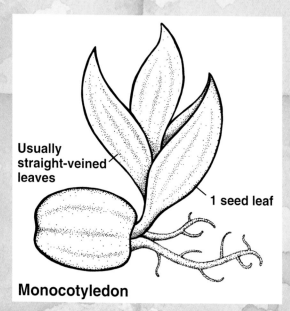

Usually straight-veined leaves

1 seed leaf

Monocotyledon

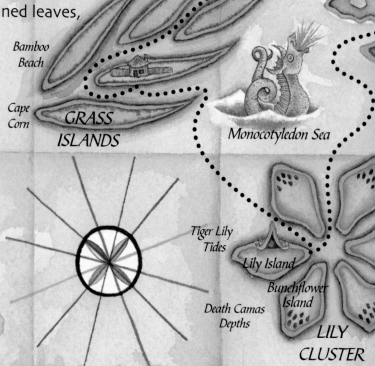

Rice Reef

Bamboo Beach

Cape Corn

GRASS ISLANDS

Monocotyledon Sea

Tiger Lily Tides

Lily Island

Bunchflower Island

Death Camas Depths

LILY CLUSTER

Botany Beaches

Savory Shoals

Chamomile Corner

Sunflower Sandbar

ASTER ARCHIPELAGO

Dandelion Delta

MINT ISLAND

Peppermint Pools

Sepal Sands

Cape Carrot

PARSLEY ISLAND

Petal Place

Weary Waves

Peach Point

PEA ISLANDS

Peanut Peninsula

Umbel Upwellings

Dill Depths

Clover Cache

Bean Bay

Blackberry Beach

Mimosa Island

Swimming Sea

Hemlock Harbor

ROSE ISLANDS

Senna Island

Horseradish Haven

MUSTARD ISLAND

Dicotyledon Sea

Guardians Gates

Swimmer's Sanctuary

Radish Reefs

Pistil Point

Stamen Stop

Lunch break

Seeds from the other islands were like the beans she collected. Plant a bean and it would unfold a leaf from each half of the seed. It was a "di-cotyle-don," meaning it had "two-seed-leaves." These plants grew mostly net-veined leaves.

The flowers were different too, Shanleya remembered. Monocots, as the people liked to say, had flowers with parts mostly in threes, while dicots had flower parts in fours and fives. The mustard flower, she recalled, had four petals and net-veined leaves, so it was a dicot. She checked the samples in her bags and all were dicots, some with separate petals and others with the petals fused together.

Now it was time to learn more about the monocots, with their straight-veined leaves and flower parts in threes. Shanleya paddled eagerly toward an area marked on the map as the Lily Cluster for her next lesson in botany.

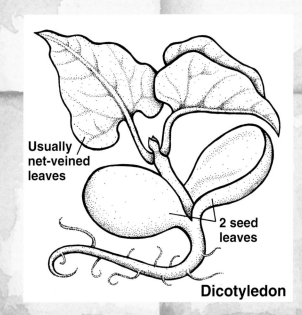

Usually net-veined leaves

2 seed leaves

Dicotyledon

NAVIGATING THE LILY CLUSTER

The Lily Cluster was a region of numerous small islands with similar characteristics. Each island was home to a different family of plants, Grandfather had explained, but they shared a lot of characteristics in common. Right away Shanleya spotted the true Lily Island with the Lily Guardian's magnificent shelter. It looked like a teepee, but it was made from an overturned lily blossom with one petal removed to make a doorway. The girl tied her canoe by the shore and hollered a friendly "Hello!" as she approached.

"Hello, hello, and hello again!" returned the Guardian, sipping from a lily cup. "What can I do for a fine young girl like yourself?"

"Would you please teach me about the Lily Family?" she asked politely.

"Very well, very well," replied the Lily Guardian merrily. "However, first you must answer one simple question. How many petals does this flower have?"

"A simple question," said the girl, "but not such a simple answer." Grandfather had taught her to start at the outside of a flower and go in by layers—first the sepals, then petals and stamens, with the pistil in the very middle. The lily looked as though it had six petals, but the first three were really sepals the same size and color as the petals. "This flower has three sepals, three petals, six stamens, and a three-parted pistil. Sometimes the sepals and petals are labeled together as six tepals," Shanleya said confidently.

"Very good, very good," said the Guardian. "If you have a flower with three sepals and three petals the same size and color, then you can bet it belongs to one of the families in the Lily Cluster, although it may be tricky to determine exactly which island it came from." The Guardian dug up a yellowbell for Shanleya to taste the starchy root, a bulb-like corm.

"Wow! This yellowbell is delicious and sweet!" she exclaimed, "but these flowers are much too pretty too dig up." Instead, they picked a small bouquet for Shanleya to take home to her mother. Then the Guardian cast lily petals out across the water, magically making a bridge to a nearby island.

"The most poisonous plants in the Lily Cluster are on Bunchflower Island," the Guardian kindly cautioned her, pointing to some death camas beside the trail. Shanleya could see where the island got its name, since the plants had bunches of little white or greenish white flowers with parts in threes.

But not all bunchflowers are poisonous, so Shanleya collected some beargrass leaves for her father to make baskets with. Then the girl and the Guardian crossed back over the bridge of Lily petals before it dissolved. She thanked him for his kindness and continued on her journey.

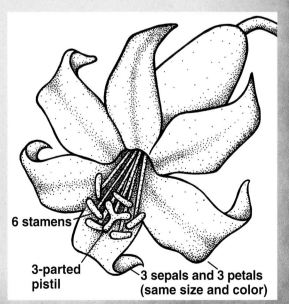

6 stamens

3-parted pistil

3 sepals and 3 petals (same size and color)

THE GRASS ISLANDS

Shanleya heard the Grass Islands before she saw them, for this was where most of the animals came to graze each day. Paddling closer, she saw wildebeasts, buffalo, gazelles, antelope, elephants, and zebras. The Grass Guardian was there too, wearing a straw hat and chewing a stalk of timothy grass as he worked in his garden. The animals didn't fear him by day, but they swam all the way back to the mainland before dark to be safe. "Howdy partner!" he greeted the girl.

"Hello," Shanleya replied. "Will you teach me about grasses?"

"There are ten thousand different species of grass. Most are small plants like these in the pasture, but others are large and woody, like this bamboo," the Guardian responded, pointing to the garden fence. His hut was also built from bamboo.

Shanleya recognized the bamboo because her people brought lots of it home to build with. "What are you growing in the garden?" she asked.

"Almost all grasses have edible seeds," the Guardian explained, "but many are small and difficult to harvest. I only plant grasses with big seeds—like wheat, oats, corn, rice, barley, millet, and rye. Let's gather some for you to take home." Together they beat the ripe seeds with a stick into a basket until it was nearly full.

Shanleya saw the Guardian slyly add some dark, dusty grass seeds into the basket. "Wait a minute!" she exclaimed, taking the basket from the Guardian. Shanleya carefully removed the bad grass seeds. "These seeds are infested with ergot fungus. Mixing them with our food could cause hallucinations and it could restrict the blood flow to our arms or legs, causing fingers and toes to die and rot!"

"I cannot fool you," he smiled. "Here is a reward for your wisdom." He gave her a big stalk of sweet sugar cane to chew on.

"Thank you," she said. "Could you show me a grass flower before I go?"

"I would be delighted to," he said and handed her a slender stem. "Grasses are wind-pollinated, so they don't need showy petals like insect-pollinated flowers. But like other true flowers, grasses do have stamens and a pistil. The flowers are enclosed in modified leaves called bracts."

Shanleya admired the dainty, easily over-looked flowers. She also remembered to examine the straight veins in the leaves. "These are monocot plants," she said to herself.

Shanleya thanked the Guardian for his help. The Grass Islands and the Lily Cluster were the only places with straight-veined leaves she would study this trip. Now she would visit more islands with the net-veined leaves of the dicot plants. With the sugar cane in her mouth, she paddled onward.

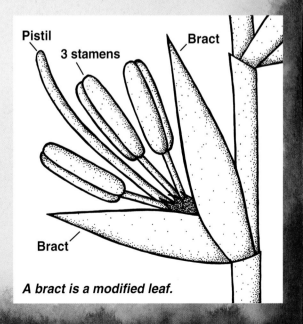

A bract is a modified leaf.

ISLANDS OF FRUITS AND ROSES

Shanleya followed the sweet smell of roses right to its source. The Rose Islands were a cluster of medium-sized islands and home to more than three thousand species of plants with rose-like flowers. "Hello!" Shanleya hollered to the Guardian as she approached. "Would you teach me about the plants of the Rose Islands?"

"Gladly," the Guardian said as he gave her a beautiful rose. "Step right up to my flower recombulator and take a look." Shanleya followed him to a giant mechanical rose. "See how there are five sepals and five petals, plus lots of stamens and pistils in the middle? That's the combination for true Roses. Now, press this magic growth button."

Shanleya did as he said, and the blossoms on the island suddenly changed, maturing into fruits right before their eyes. They were surrounded by rose hips, strawberries, blackberries, and raspberries. "You know, all these berries would just get mashed in my collecting bag," Shanleya said, eating as many as she could without saving any.

When Shanleya was finally full, the Guardian asked, "Ready for a new combination?" They removed most of the stamens and all but one pistil, until the flower recombulator looked like a plum blossom. Suddenly they appeared on Plum Island. Shanleya eagerly pressed the magic button and watched as apricots, cherries, nectarines, peaches, and plums ripened from flowers into fruits. "A fruit is like a pregnant woman," the Guardian said. "After being fertilized with pollen from the male stamens, the baby grows inside the womb of the pistil. It is truly a baby plant, with the beginnings of a root and leaves, but we call them 'seeds.'"

"Now here is one very pregnant-looking peach," Shanleya observed as she filled her bag. "Hey, all of these fruits have a seam down one side and a hard pit in the middle."

"That is a good pattern for the fruits of Plum Island," the Guardian said. "But did you also notice how these fruits form on top of the flower, instead of underneath?" He pushed the pistil dowin in the recombulator until it was beneath the petals and sepals, then put back some of the stamens, instantly transporting them to Apple Island. Shanleya pushed the growth button and the flowers quickly matured into apples, pears and all kinds of berries. Only this time the fruits swelled up beneath the flowers. On the end of each fruit was a little five-pointed star made from what used to be sepals around the blossom.

Numerous stamens

5 petals

5 sepals

"If the pistil is attached below the sepals and petals," the Guardian said, "then the fruit forms below the flower too." Shanleya's bag grew heavy with the delicious fruit. Finally, they reset the flower recombulator for Rose Island and returned to Shanleya's canoe. "Thanks for your kindness. I will think of you as I savor these fruits at home," the girl promised as she left.

THE ASTER ARCHIPELAGO

"Father Sun," Shanleya said out loud as she paddled, "you are looking tired, resting there on the horizon, and you are not as hot as you were a few hours ago." The girl knew that night was coming soon, but she still had one more place to go to complete Grandfather's instructions. "Your last stop," he had said, "will be the Aster Archipelago. You should know this family well. There are more than 19,000 different species there."

Ahead Shanleya could see a tight group of islands. She chose one to land on, tied her canoe securely, and walked onshore. The trail was littered with sunflower seed shells, and near the trail was one big, beautiful sunflower in full bloom. Shanleya buried her nose in the flower to smell it, then shrieked and jumped back when the sunflower opened his eyes. It was the Guardian of the Aster Islands, and he laughed and laughed. "Excuse me," he finally said. "I was just napping here, soaking up the warm afternoon sun. How can I help you?"

"Could you please teach me about the Asters?" Shanleya asked politely.

"Of course," said the Guardian, "but first I have a test for you. Answer correctly, and I will share everything I know. Answer incorrectly, and I will cast a spell to make you forever confused and befuddled. How many petals do members of the Aster Family have?" He motioned to the ring of thirty or so yellow petal-like parts around his face.

"The Asters are composite flowers," Shanleya answered. "One flowerhead is composed of many smaller flowers on a single disc in a way that looks like one big flower," she continued. "Look closely at the little flowers of the disc and you will see that each has five tiny petals, all fused together around the stamens and pistil. The big 'petals' around the outside are really 'ray flowers.' Each petal is a flower by itself, with its petals fused together and stretched out to one side. So the correct answer is five," she finished.

"Girl, that was a mouthful," said the Guardian. "But you are correct, so let's look around." One island was home to plants with dandelion-like flowers, which had no disc flowers, just ray flowers overlapping from the middle outward. A lettuce blossom looks almost identical to a dandelion. "Plants with dandelion-like flowers are edible, though some are bitter," the Guardian nearly growled.

Shanleya noticed his changing mood. "I don't have much time before dark," she thought. She gathered a supply of sunflower seeds, aromatic chamomile for tea, and sagebrush to make the lodge smell good. Night was coming quickly now, and the Guardian kept pausing to sniff the air and growl. He seemed to be changing right before her eyes. Shanleya walked away as if she were looking for herbs, but only until she was safely out of sight. Quickly and quietly, she ran for the canoe and paddled out of harm's way.

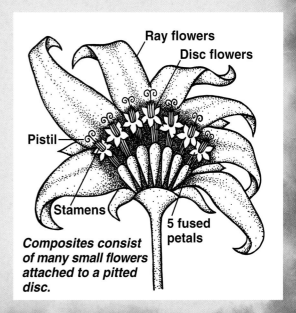

Ray flowers
Disc flowers
Pistil
Stamens
5 fused petals

Composites consist of many small flowers attached to a pitted disc.

END OF THE GREAT TREE

Shanleya steered her canoe towards home and paddled hard, eager to be back in her Grandfather's arms. A few miles out she met the great herd of animals swimming back to shore for the night. Carefully she paddled through the herd, then led the pack on the journey for land. She paddled until all the color was gone from the sky, as Father Sun pulled the blankets over his head. But Mother Moon kept the nightlight on, and the girl kept paddling. "Thank you for watching over me," she said gratefully.

By the dim light Shanleya could make out the peaks of her homeland on the low horizon. This last part of the journey seemed to last forever. It had been so much easier paddling the other way early in the morning while she was fresh and full of energy. Now she was exhausted, but kept paddling until it seemed like she was paddling in her sleep. Finally nodding over, she nearly tipped right out of the canoe!

Wide awake from the jolt, the girl caught a faint flicker of light on the land ahead. It was Grandfather keeping a fire going on the beach to guide her home. With renewed strength, Shanleya paddled furiously the rest of the way to shore and leaped out of the canoe to give Grandfather a hug. "You have done well, Granddaughter," he said. "I am so proud of you."

The two unloaded the bounty of fruits and vegetables from her collecting bags and carried the canoe up the beach above the tide. At last Shanleya tumbled into her bed and fell into a deep, deep sleep.

"Is that the end of the story?" The children asked the gray-haired old woman as she reached for another piece of wood to put on the fire. "Please, Grandmother," they begged, "will you tell us more?"

"No, and yes," Grandmother replied, chuckling at their youthful energy. "Shanleya grew up to be a great botanist. By the time she was a grown woman with children of her own, it was said that she knew more about the plants and how to use them than anyone else among our people."

"So, whatever happened to the Great Tree?" Adelia wondered. "The world isn't like that now."

"No, the world has changed. That is true," the old woman said. "Shanleya was on the islands with her children the day the Great Tree fell. An earthquake knocked them right to the ground, then the islands just crumbled and sank out of sight below. She barely made it back to the canoe with her children."

"Father Sun heard her call for help," she continued. "After all those billions of years of waiting and watching their little Earth grow up, he couldn't stand to see everything lost on the ocean floor. In one big gulp Father Sun drained the oceans to where they are today. The fossilized trunk of the Great Tree was scattered in millions of pieces across the land, and the living plants took root where they fell."

"But won't the earth flood again in Time?" Peter asked.

"No," replied Grandmother. "Something had to be done, but Father Sun couldn't just get rid of Time. After all, the plants needed Time to grow, " she said, pouring each of the children a cup of the cold, clear liquid, "and so do you."

"To fix the problem," she went on, "Father Sun made Time so that with his great warmth it would evaporate from the oceans to be used again. Time is invisible on its way up into the sky. There it condenses into great clouds that carry it over land, where it falls again. Drip-drop, drip-drop, it is always raining Time somewhere in the world."

"Grandmother," asked Katlyn, sitting beside Peter, "how can we possibly learn about the plants like Shanleya did, now that they are all mixed up on the ground?"

"Easy. You can still identify plants by the same patterns Shanleya used. The Mints have square stems and opposite leaves, and most of them smell minty. The Mustards can be identified wherever you are, as long as you remember the secret combination. The same is true for all the other families of plants and their patterns. It is like a great treasure hunt to go out and search for the plants that match the patterns. All you have to do is look."

"That's how I learned about plants as a girl," the old woman continued. "I went on walks with Great-Grandmother Shanleya. She would show me the family patterns, then send me ahead to search for flowers that fit the patterns. Great-Grandmother walked along slowly behind me, always picking at rocks in the ground. Sometimes she found fossils from the Great Tree, and she usually knew something about how those ancient plants were related to the ones we have today."

"But what happened to the Guardians?" asked Peter.

"Oh, the Guardians are still out there," cautioned Grand-mother. "They are the protectors of the plants. Fortunately, they will not bother you as long as you remember the patterns and play by the rules. It is only when you try something foolish, like eating a plant you do not know, that you are in real danger."

"Now Grandchildren," she said a bit wearily, "it is late and time for bed. Tomorrow will bring a bright new day. We can go for a walk and you can show me everything you know about the flowers. Until then, good night."